P9-DEG-932

Kobe Bryant

Revised Edition

By Jeff Savage

AMAZING
ATHLETES

Lerner Publications Company • Minneapolis

Copyright © 2011 by Jeff Savage

Lerner Publications Company
A division of Lerner Publishing Group, Inc.
241 First Avenue North
Minneapolis, MN 55401 U.S.A.

Website address: www.lernerbooks.com

Library of Congress Cataloging-in-Publication Data

Savage, Jeff, 1961–
        Kobe Bryant / by Jeff Savage. — Rev. ed.
            p.   cm. — (Amazing athletes)
        Includes bibliographical references and index.
        ISBN 978-0-7613-5752-0 (pbk. : alk. paper)
        1. Bryant, Kobe, 1978–—Juvenile literature. 2. Basketball players—United States—Biography—Juvenile literature. 3. Los Angeles Lakers (Basketball team)—Juvenile literature. I. Title.
    GV884.B794S273 2011
    796.323'092—dc22 [B]   2009035646

Manufactured in the United States of America
1 – BP – 7/15/10

TABLE OF CONTENTS

Kobe Bryant dribbles past Orlando Magic player Mickael Pietrus.

BACK ON TOP

The heat was on for **shooting guard** Kobe Bryant and the Los Angeles Lakers. Only a few minutes were left in the fourth **quarter**. The Lakers were counting on their best player to win the game.

Kobe and the Lakers were playing in the 2009 National Basketball Association (NBA) **Finals**. They had already won three games in the series against the Orlando Magic. They needed just one more win to become NBA champions.

Lakers' fans celebrate during the 2009 NBA Finals.

Kobe works hard to get the ball to the basket.

Kobe plays his best basketball when it matters most. He knew that he could lead the Lakers to victory. "I was just completely locked in," he said after the game.

The Lakers had been ahead for most of the game. But the Magic would not give up. Kobe knew that he had to keep working hard in the fourth quarter.

Kobe took a **pass** far from the basket. He jumped off the floor just behind the **three-point line** and let go of the ball. Kobe's **jump shot** sailed through the basket. Los Angeles was ahead by 16 points. Orlando was forced to call a **timeout** as the Lakers celebrated.

The Magic would not be able to catch up. Los Angeles was ahead when the game ended, 99–86. The Lakers were champions of the NBA!

Kobe celebrates at the end of the game.

This was the fourth NBA championship for Kobe. But this victory was special. The Lakers had lost the NBA Finals to the Boston Celtics in 2008. Kobe was happy to get back to the Finals and win the series. "It felt so good to be able to have this moment," Kobe said after the game.

Kobe holds up four fingers. This was Kobe's fourth NBA championship.

As a kid, Kobe watched his dad, Joe "Jellybean" Bryant, play professional basketball.

A BROAD EDUCATION

Kobe Bryant learned the sport of basketball as a young boy. Kobe's father, Joe, played 16 years as a professional, eight in the NBA. Joe's nickname was "Jellybean," because a fan once gave him jelly beans.

Kobe was born August 23, 1978, into a close family. His mother, Pam, and his older sisters, Sharia and Shaya, are among his most supportive fans.

When Kobe was three, he began watching his father play basketball on television. Kobe put his little hoop next to the TV and watched his father shoot the basketball. Then Kobe would shoot his foam basketball at his hoop, pretending to be just like dad. In 1984, Kobe's father left the NBA to join a professional league in Europe. Kobe packed his basketball and hoop and his other belongings and moved with his family to Italy.

Kobe's middle name is Bean, which is short for "Jellybean."

Kobe already spoke English, of course. He learned to speak Italian in school. At home,

The Bryant family lived in Pistoia, Italy, while Joe was playing for the European leagues. During his stay, Kobe practiced his basketball skills.

he practiced new Italian words with his sisters at the kitchen table.

Kobe also practiced basketball. He would **dribble** and shoot every day at the school playground. But in Europe, soccer is much more popular than basketball. So when the other children arrived with a soccer ball, Kobe had to put his basketball away.

Kobe has said his parents encouraged him to be an individual. "They taught me that there would be criticisms. . . , but you've just got to do what you think is right."

When Kobe was eight, he started going to his father's pro basketball practices. Kobe sometimes practiced with the team. He learned to make smart passes and be a good teammate. The Italian players had fun playing with Kobe.

In 1991, when Kobe was 13, he and his family returned to the United States. They lived near Philadelphia, Pennsylvania. Kobe spoke proper English, which he had learned from textbooks. Many American boys spoke **slang**. It was difficult for Kobe to understand their words. He was even teased. Playing basketball helped Kobe make friends.

By the time Kobe was at Lower Merion High School, his basketball skills were already well above those of his classmates.

HIGH SCHOOL STAR

Kobe studied hard and earned good grades during his four years at Lower Merion High School in Pennsylvania. He was an instant star for the school basketball team, the Aces.

Kobe wowed crowds with his quickness, strength, and drive to get the ball to the basket.

In one game, he had the flu but played anyway and led the Aces to a victory. In another, he made 9 of 10 second-half shots to pull off an amazing comeback win. He could play any position. But he mostly played point guard so that he could dribble the ball for his team.

Kobe's father once played for the NBA's Philadelphia 76ers. In 1994, Joe Bryant asked the 76ers coach to allow Kobe to practice with the team. The coach kindly agreed. Kobe was just 16. But he was able to keep up with the pro players. In fact, sometimes he was the best player on the court.

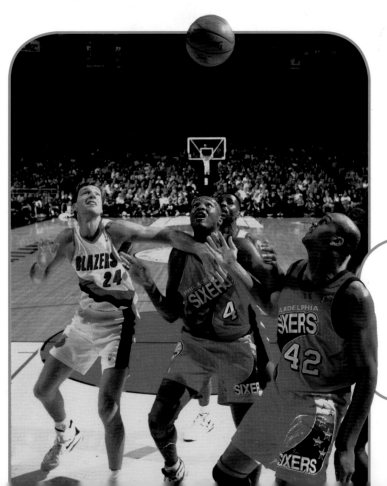

The Philadelphia 76ers (here playing against the Portland Trailblazers) allowed Kobe to practice with them in the mid-1990s. Kobe was still in high school!

Kobe led his Lower Merion team to the 1996 state championship.

Michael Jordan is widely thought to be the greatest basketball player ever. Even in high school, though, people whispered that Kobe might someday become as great as Jordan.

As a senior in high school, Kobe averaged 31 points, 12 **rebounds**, and 7 **assists** per game. He led Lower Merion to a 31–3 record and the Pennsylvania state title. He finished his four years of high school as the leading scorer in southern Pennsylvania history. He broke the 1950s record of the great Wilt Chamberlain.

Wilt Chamberlain shows off his big hands. He was a star basketball player in high school, college, and the NBA.

Colleges around the country invited Kobe to play for their basketball team. Kobe had good grades. He was talented enough to go to the college of his choice. But Kobe announced that he was available for the 1996 NBA **draft**. Every summer, all the pro teams take turns picking two promising players each. Most of the players chosen have attended college. Kobe was about to become just the seventh player in 30 years to go straight from high school to the NBA.

In April 1996, at his high school gym, Kobe announced that he was going straight to the NBA.

The Charlotte Hornets drafted Kobe in 1996. He was later traded to the Los Angeles Lakers.

A KID IN A MAN'S GAME

The Charlotte Hornets selected Kobe with the 13th pick in the 1996 draft. Other teams were interested in him too. The Los Angeles Lakers offered to trade **veteran** center Vlade Divac to the Hornets in exchange for Kobe. The Hornets accepted the offer. Kobe became a member of the Lakers.

Kobe signed a three-year **contract** with the Lakers for $3.5 million. Kobe and his family moved west to Los Angeles. With some of the money, Kobe bought a big house in a wealthy area. The house was roomy enough for the family to live together. Kobe's bedroom overlooked the Pacific Ocean and downtown Los Angeles.

After the trade, Kobe moved to Los Angeles. He enjoyed hanging out with his family and friends in his new house.

Kobe had a lot to learn about playing at the NBA level.

Kobe had grown to six feet seven inches. He could shoot, pass, dribble, and rebound well enough to play any position. He usually played guard.

Kobe was barely 18 years old when he became the youngest player ever to play in an NBA game. Against the Minnesota Timberwolves, Kobe played six minutes of the game. He missed one shot, made one rebound, and had one **block**.

Crowds at the All-Star Game in early 1997 cheered Kobe's slam dunks. He won the annual contest.

Kobe learned plenty as a **rookie**, and he began to play more minutes each game. His favorite part of the season was the All-Star Game. He won the slam dunk contest.

Kobe was much younger than his teammates. Things weren't always easy for him. After games, Kobe's teammates would go out to nightclubs. Kobe would go home. In his free time, he'd hang out with his sisters.

Kobe continued to practice and improve. He wasn't a **starter** on the Lakers yet. In fact, one of his first NBA starts came in the 1998 NBA All-Star Game. Fans across the country had voted to see Kobe play. He even got to play with the great Michael Jordan.

Kobe put on quite a show at the All-Star Game. He scored a team-high 18 points with a variety of hard-to-make shots. Kobe became a starter on the Lakers soon after.

Kobe and Shaquille O'Neal were two of the Lakers' top players.

LAKER LEADER

Kobe quickly became a star. He was scoring 20 points or more in games. He was making smart passes to his teammates and playing sticky defense.

At first, Kobe and center Shaquille O'Neal competed with each other more than they helped each other on the court. Eventually, though, they developed into a dynamic duo. The Lakers beat the Indiana Pacers in the 2000 NBA Finals to win the title. They won their second straight world championship in 2001 by defeating the Philadelphia 76ers. The Lakers' third straight title in 2002 was a 4–0 defeat of the New Jersey Nets.

Kobe has been making news off the court as well. In 2001, he married Vanessa Laine. Their first child was born in 2003. (A second baby arrived in 2006.)

In 2003, the Lakers lost to the San Antonio Spurs in the playoffs. The Spurs would go on to win the NBA championship. Los Angeles was back in the Finals in 2004 against the Detroit Pistons. But the Pistons played tough defense. They beat the Lakers 4 games to 1.

Kobe dribbles past his former teammate Shaq during a game against the Miami Heat.

Kobe and Shaq were both disappointed about losing in the Finals. Shaq decided he would be better off on a different team. He asked to be traded. The Lakers agreed and sent Shaq to the Miami Heat. With Shaq gone, Kobe became the leader of the Lakers. He was ready for the challenge. But would Los Angeles be good enough to get back to the Finals without Shaq?

The Lakers struggled at first. They did not make the playoffs at all in 2005. In 2006 they lost in the first round to the Phoenix Suns. The Suns beat the Lakers again in the first round of the 2007 playoffs.

Kobe was frustrated. He felt his team was not good enough to win the championship again. To make the team better, the Lakers traded for Pau Gasol in 2008. Gasol had been a star for the Memphis Grizzlies. The move paid off. The Lakers returned to the Finals in 2008. They lost to the tough defense of the Celtics. In 2009, Kobe and Gasol led their team back to the Finals. This time, they would not be stopped, beating the Magic in five games.

Kobe gets a hug from Pau Gasol after winning the 2009 NBA Finals.

Kobe is already one of the most successful players in the history of the NBA. "I want to be," he says, "the best player who ever set foot on a basketball court." With four world championships and counting, Kobe just might reach his goal.

Kobe *(holding daughter Gianna)* and his wife, Vanessa *(beside daughter Natalia)*, celebrate during the Lakers' victory parade in 2009.

Selected Career Highlights

2008-2009   was third in the NBA in scoring with 26.8 points per game
won his fourth NBA Championship

2007-2008   was second in the NBA in scoring with 28.3 points per game

2006-2007   led the NBA in scoring with 32.8 points per game

2005-2006   led the NBA in scoring with 35.4 points per game

2004-2005   was second in the NBA in scoring with 27.6 points per game

2003-2004   scored 20 points in the NBA All-Star Game

2002-2003   named to the All-NBA First Team
received most votes in NBA All-Star ballot
made record-breaking 12 three-pointers
  in a single game
became the youngest player in NBA history
  to reach 10,000 points for his career

2001-2002   named to the All-NBA First Team
won his third NBA Championship

2000-2001   named to the All-NBA Second Team
won his second NBA Championship

1999-2000   named to the All-NBA Second Team
won his first NBA Championship

1998-1999   named to the All-NBA Third Team

1997-1998   became the youngest player ever to start in the
NBA All-Star Game

1996-1997   became the youngest player ever to play in an NBA game
won the NBA slam dunk contest at the All-Star Game
set the NBA All-Star Rookie Game scoring record with 31 points
named National High School Player of the Year

Glossary

assists: a pass of the ball to a teammate so the teammate can score

block: a strike of the ball to stop an opponent's shot from going in the hoop

contract: a written deal signed by a player and his or her team. The player agrees to play for the team for a stated number of years. The team agrees to pay the player a stated amount of money.

draft: a yearly event in which professional teams in a sport are given the chance to pick new players from a selected group. Most of the players in the group have played their sport in college.

dribble: to continuously bounce a ball, using one hand

Finals: the NBA's championship series. The team that wins four games in the series becomes the NBA champion.

jump shot: a shot of any length in which a player jumps in the air before shooting the ball over a defender

pass: a throw or bounce of the basketball to a teammate to move the ball closer to the basket

quarter: one of four periods in a basketball game

rebound: the catch of a ball off the hoop or the backboard after a shot has been missed

rookie: a player who is playing his or her first season

shooting guard: a player on a basketball team who is responsible for scoring points. Shooting guards are skilled at dribbling and shooting the ball.

slang: words that are playful or odd, but not proper grammar

starter: a person who is named to play from the beginning of the game

three-point line: a curved line, or arc, on the floor at each end of the court. Shots made from outside this line are worth three points.

timeout: a period when a team can stop play for a short time. In the NBA, each team gets six timeouts per game.

veteran: a player who has played more than one season. A player is usually called a veteran after he or she has played several seasons.

Further Reading & Websites

Bernstein, Ross. *Shaquille O'Neal*. Minneapolis: Lerner Publications Company, 2009.

Stewart, Mark. *Kobe Bryant: Hard to the Hoop*. Minneapolis: Millbrook Press, 2000.

Stewart, Mark, and Mike Kennedy. *Swish: The Quest for Basketball's Perfect Shot*. Minneapolis: Millbrook Press, 2009.

Taylor, Trace. *Basketball*. Philadelphia: ARC Press, 2009.

Los Angeles Lakers Website
http://www.nba.com/lakers
The official website of the Lakers includes team schedules, late-breaking news, profiles of past and present players, and much more.

Official NBA Website
http://www.nba.com
A website developed by the National Basketball Association (NBA) that provides fans with recent news stories, statistics, biographies of players and coaches, and information about games.

Sports Illustrated Kids
http://www.sikids.com
The *Sports Illustrated Kids* website that covers all sports, including basketball.

Index

Photo Acknowledgments

The images in this book are used with the permission of: REUTERS/Jeff
Haynes, p. 4; AP Photo/David J. Phillip, p. 5; AP Photo/Stan Honda, Pool,
p. 6; AP Photo/John Raoux, pp. 7, 27; REUTERS/Kevin Kolczynksi, p. 8;
© Bettmann/CORBIS, pp. 9, 17; © Michael Freeman/CORBIS, p. 11; © Jay
Gorodetzer/CORBIS, pp. 13, 16; © Jay Gorodetzer, p. 14; © Brian Drake/
Time & Life Pictures/Getty Images, p. 15; AP Photo/Rusty Kennedy, p. 18; AP
Photo/Susan Sterner, p. 19; © Neal Preston/CORBIS, p. 20; © David Taylor/
Allsport/Getty Images, p. 21; © Brian Bahr/Allsport/Getty Images, p. 22;
REUTERS/Lucy Nicholson, p. 24; © Lisa Blumenfeld/Getty Images, p. 26; AP
Photo/Richard Vogel, p. 28; REUTERS/Adrees Latif, p. 29.

Cover: © Donald Page Southcreek Sports/Icon SMI

10/10